WITH
THE
LAMP
TURNED
LOW

Poems By John Muller

Published by Piscataqua Press

An imprint of RiverRun Bookstore, Inc.

32 Daniel Street

Portsmouth, NH 03801

www.riverrunbookstore.com

www.piscataquapress.com

ISBN: 978-1-950381-56-2

Printed in the United States of America

for Pete Devlin

fellow poet and

my great, good friend

Sounding

I whisper my prayers
hoping they will fall
softly and
to such a depth
to be able
to distinguish
my own echo from
that which I wish
to fathom.

An Orange Study

I lay
on the couch
considering

suggestions

of a room
illumined with
the light of
a solitary
jack-o-lantern

A Constant Shadow

There is always
this Puritan standing
behind me when,
reading,
I sit and rock.

Stern of face he looks
over my shoulder
taking
the dark view
of those things
that interest me.

The Empty Mirror

I sit near
the window that
looks out upon
the yard and
the trees beyond.

I sit here
calm and
determined
to see what is left
of the day into
darkness.

In one hand I hold
a book which
I have read often,
one which
gives me comfort
just to hold.

In the other I hold
my glasses which
at times
look as if
they belong to
someone else.

How easily
this room
takes to darkness.

How simply
it accepts
the cold.

I draw my chair
closer to
the window.

There is less of
yard and
trees now.

The sky beyond
recedes.

Soon I will sit
in darkness
looking out and
seeing neither
reflection
nor beyond.

His Room

It is to this
back attic room that
he comes to when
the moon is full and
the others sleep.

It is beyond
its one window that
the highest branches
of the old oak
sway slowly.

It is here when
all is *just so* that
he comes to trace
shadows
on a bare wall.

Survivor

By this moon's
sudden appearance
I see that the storm
has moved off.

On my face
the touch of
the faint snow
that still
fills the air.

Standing there I find
that nothing
compels.

And now I know
what it takes
to survive in
a changed and
changing world.

And now I know that
that
is all I need
to know.

Taken

With the weight of
its own inevitability
night begins to fill
this quiet corner
of the woods.

These sullen trees
this ice bound brook
this single
outcropping
of granite
succumb and I

wait
on its silence
ready
to be taken,

ready to be
someone different
from he who came
slowly drawn
by last light.

Traces Of Snow

I have let
the aurochs loose.

It is empty now
here
in the barn and
it smells of
late winter rain.

These old stones
and these beams
now gone to rot
know more of
years of
hard weather
than of beast.

I stand where once
there was a door
and watch the fog
drift down from
the highlands.

In silence
the stone walls
the fields of
rock
mud and
pale dead grass
fade to
a gray nothing.

I have let
the aurochs loose
at last and

they have gone
up there to
the pasture beyond
the last stone wall,

up to where
there are still
traces of snow.

Going Once More

Once again
I have come
to stare down
into it.

Once again
I have come
to measure
the emptiness.

This pile of dirt
here beside me
appears to be
so much less than
what has been
emptied.

This shovel
I have used
too often.

Today I will
use it for
the last time.

Now I know that
this is as deep
as it can ever get.

Today
the flowers left
no longer
comfort me.

Today I note
their lack
of roots.

Today
the trees along
the stone wall
stand still and
empty.

Today
I know that I
have come here
too often and
enough.

From here on in
all of this will be
someone else's burden.

Lifetime

As always
I stand with
my back to
time.

Behind me
the rope
burns slowly
knot
by knot.

Deeply and with
measured breaths
I inhale
its incense as

I stare ahead
into an
emptiness
that I know
can only be
endless.

As always
I stand
longing to take
that one last step,

but I
content myself
to wait until
nothing
is left of time
but ash.

Darkness

It comes on
so easily

like a drawer
gently shut

or a lid
slowly lowered.

It is never
new.

It is always
somewhere

and so near
that I only
have to close
my eyes to
find it.

Hello Again

Hello
so soon
again.

Each cycle
seems to turn
more tightly
as we go on.

Except for that
there is nothing
all that different as,
from the first,
our knowledge
was complete.

As grim a comfort
as that may be
and is
it is a comfort
nevertheless,

and so with that
and with calm
and quiet

we cycle through.

Hello
yet again.

Apotheosis

One now with
the wind
and able
to raise
sand enough
to blot out
the sun

or

to carry
the fragrance of
a land loved
to one where
nothing abides.

One now with
the wind,
a soul freed
and not
to be denied.

One now with
the wind,
able to
caress the wings
of fallen angels.

Thief

There you sit
naked
with a cigarette.

That's you
thief enough to
steal all that
kept me from
desire.

That's you
expert criminal,
leaving nothing but
the fragrant allure
of the theft.

That's you
so lovely and
naked
with a cigarette.

Before First Snow

It would be these
last few apples,
left unpicked, from
this leafless tree that
I would wish
for you.

Here to this field
turned and
turned away from
for the last time
before first snow
I have come.

Here to this
stone wall
ready to stand
witness to
another winter
I have come.

Here I have come
to say your name
once more
at last light and
watch my breath
rise up and
disappear
as easily as
this day
slips away
into night.

Recital

This night he avoids
the light that falls
from her window.
This night he keeps
to the dark as
he and the dog
cross the yard.

This night he notices
the light rain
on his face
as he heads for
the tall pine at
the edge of
the wood where
it is even
darker still.

Stepping
in beneath it
he stops
and turns back
to look across
to where he is not.

The dog
comes up and
stands beside him.

From here there is
nothing of the house
but window and
within.

From here
he can see her
at the piano,
her back straight
her eyes
on the music
before her.

It is a duet
that he hears,
one of piano
and light rain
on fallen leaves.

The melody is one
of earth
not yet frozen
and the smell
of wet dog.

As he stands there
and listens,
a car approaches
its headlights bright
on wet pavement.

Watching it pass,
he pulls back in
closer beneath
the pine hoping,
within its presence,
to listen
more unseen
than ever.

Parallax

Waking
she found
the room
bathed
in light.

Turning
to the window
she found
the moon
full over
November trees.

Rolling on
to her back
she found
the bed
half empty.

Outside,
looking up at
the same window
he saw
only the moon's
reflection.

Still

I do not know
how long I was
gone out there.

Long enough
to see the last
house lights
swallowed up
by the night.

Long enough
to see
every star
happen.

Long enough
to grow cold
and then
to grow
used to
the cold.

Without
forethought I
said your name
and my breath
rose up before me
and disappeared.

I said it again
without voice
but with intent
as I would
utter something
hallowed.

When I did
I looked up
just in time
to see
the stars fall
in silence.

They fell beyond
the far hills
where I
have never been
leaving me with
nothing save
the night.

How long?

I do not know.

I only know
that later
I found myself
lying by your side
in our small room
and beyond
the window
there was
first light.

Morning Snow

Beyond
the bedroom window
there is
snow falling
and silence.

She lies beside me
her face
turned away.

Lying there
I study
the graceful line
of her neck
and shoulder,
the smoothness
of her skin,
the gray hair
woven in with
the brown.

Keeping still
I try to measure
just how blessed I am
to have been with
and to still be with
someone who will
at times
turn away
to the window
to where snow falls
to the silence.

Kept

Not for
the few ounces
gold and

not for
the names entered
and registered

or the words
spoken and
witnessed.

None of that
has
or ever could
hold,

and yet
held it has
and does

for a heart that
cannot keep to
itself or
from going
back to and
through again
the matters
of the heart,

for a heart that
insists upon
repeating itself
to itself.

Attending

I will
wait for you in
the night when
the moon is
bright upon
the snow.

If you come
we shall go.

I will
wait for you by
the ancient oak,
and I will wear
its shadow
for a cloak.

It will be so that
if you come
we shall go.

I will
wait for you
whenever
the moon is full.

When you feel
its pull you
will know that
I have come and
we can go.

A Place To Stop

The fountain
silent now and
littered with
dry leaves.

Above us
a sky of
low gray
admits nothing.

Cold,
and our hands have
grown familiar
with our pockets
and nothing else.

The coats we wear
smell of
an empty closet in
an empty room.

Side by side
we stand trying
to think of
that which isn't
anymore.

Side by side
we stand
putting off
the long walk
back down
the empty streets.

This Desert

This is a desert
where no shadows
abide.

This is a desert
where the wind
blows bitter,
harsh and
without end.

This is a desert
where the sand
lies coarse
and cold.

It is here
that I came
to and never
turned back from.

It is to here
that,
without being
beckoned,
you followed.

Turn now and see
how there are no
footprints
leading back to
the last oasis.

Derelict

We came upon it
far from
the main channel
where the wide, flat
salt marsh
finally yields
to solid ground.

We came upon it
by following
a narrow creek
carved in mud
by fresh run-off
and tide.

Well in
from the bay
well in
from anywhere
navigable,
it lay leaning
to one side
among high,
dry reeds that
swayed with the
winter wind.

An open vessel
with the smallest
cuddy cabin,
its planking
and ribs a
pale gray now
and dry as bone.
We examined it
carefully with
an eye for
damage but
found none.

With our
combined weight
on one side
the other,
to our surprise,
rose easily.
There was really
that little to it.
Upon release
it slowly
settled back.

The earth,
soft with
salt grass
on mud, gave
to our steps

as we made
our way to
the stern,
only to find
no name across
the transom.

Laying a hand
on it for
support,
she turned
to look back out
over the salt marsh.
Watching her,
I waited.

"Was there a storm?"
she asked
her eyes still
elsewhere.

"A hurricane,
when I was
barely old
enough to
remember."

Steadying herself,
she rose up
on her toes.
"I can't see the bay."

"No, not from
down here, but
it is there
just the same."

"Yes, I'm sure
that it is."

Far off on
the other side
of the marsh
seagulls swarmed
over a landfill.

Farther off still
refinery tanks
stood out white
against a clear,
blue sky like
Alexandria
in the time of
plague.

"Is there anything else?"

I thought of
a duck blind
and a road
seldom used now
that led through
scrub trees to
a small sand pit
and no further.

I thought of spent
shotgun shells
treadless tires
twists of fence
and rusting
metal drums.

I thought of how
things can last
long after they are
abandoned.

"C'mon," I said
scrambling up onto
the roof of
the cuddy cabin.
"Up here."

She followed
and we stood
taking in
all that
there was
to be seen.

"There," she said,
pointing off
to the east.

Yes, there,
beyond the marsh
in all its vastness.
Yes, there,
as far away
as anything.
"Yes there,
white caps and
blue water.
Yes there,
clouds
high and white
racing away with
the wind.

"Yes," I said,
"and you can
almost hear the
horseshoe crabs
coupling."

"Almost."

Slide

I have this color
transparency
of you sitting
in the dunes by
a March sea
twisting a blade
of beach grass
into nothing as
you stare into
the opaque sand
straining
not to see
what
will happen next.

The crash
of the surf
on the jetty is
relentless.

The wearing away
of the shore is
inevitable.

The nature of
all things will
undermine your
hand-cup cradle
of sand and
everything
will slide
into the sea
grain by grain.

Menemsha

Both daughter and I
keep an eye out for
footholds of shade as
we make our way
barefoot along
the dock where
the fishing and
lobster boats
tie up.

These boards
beneath our feet
are as much
sand and
salt and
sun and
the footsteps of
fishermen as
they are of wood.

We walk this often
eyeing the daily catch
baskets of lobster
claws banded or pegged
buckets of fish and
fish too large
for a bucket.

We walk this way often
taking stock of
stacks of
lobster pots, piles
of nets that
await repair,
net markers and
buoys leaning
against gray shacks.

We walk this way often
avoiding broken shells
and steering clear of
small boys with their
poles and hooks.

We walk this often
and read the names
of the idle boats:
The Unicorn
The Mary Elizabeth
The Carol L.

"The Katie M.,"
I said one time,
"would be a good one."

I turned expecting
to see her
bright smile.
I was not
disappointed.

We often stop
at dock's end
just
to pause before
returning, and
often, as
naturally as
the tide turns,
her hand
finds mine,

hands that
at that moment,
are as much
sea and
sand and sun
as they are of
anything else.

(for Kate)

Long Pond

At the pond's edge
in the wet sand where
the imprints of
my daughter's feet
end

I stop.

Behind me
the sand is
hot with sun,
and too dry for
footprints to take.

Beyond that
there is nothing
but ocean
beneath nothing
but sky.

"Watch,"
she says
turning and
already
knee deep.

Reaching high,
she arcs forward
into dark water.

Arms,
head,
back,
legs,
and then
feet
and then
nothing,

nothing but
water all
the darker for
her absence.

A long moment later
surfacing further out
she turns to me
treading water and
smiling beneath
wet hair.

"It drops off
sooo
quickly.

"I wanted you
to see.

"It's
sooo
deep.

"I can't even
find the bottom."

All I can do
is nod,
just nod.

"Can I swim?"
she asks as
she begins to
scull away.

"You better,"
I say.
"You better."

(for Sarah)

Starfish

Here in the shallows,
the sand between these
large, dark rocks
swirls
with each gentle
inundation.

It is here
that starfish
can be found.

Knee deep, with
a slight breeze
playing on our
fine hairs, we
handle them with
as much care
as we would
ourselves.

They are pink
beige and
flecked with
black.

They go well
with the cliffs of
clay that
tower
over us.

They are firm
yet supple,
and wet,
and know,
like our own
naked selves,
the sea.

They are of
a species far
different from
those found
dry to death
on the lobster pots
stacked on
the high docks, or

for sale in
small baskets in
small shops up
and beyond
the cliffs.

With these
we take
no step away.

With these
we go
nowhere else.

These we will
lower and
lay back on
the soft swirling
sand between
the large, dark
rocks.

They will
remain
just where
they were
as our
naked selves
wade in to shore.

Beach Walk

Late now and
the light low.

Before us
our shadows
lengthen
along the sand.

I reach and,
far ahead,
one hand takes
another and
is taken.

Theirs

They took
their sense of
eternity
with them.
It was

as fragrant as
sea air

as constant as
the light waves
that roll onto
soft sand

as impenetrable as
the fog that lay
around them

as unseen as
one seagull
crying somewhere
up above,

and kept it
for far longer
than it takes
to create
a gem from
a fragment of
broken glass.

Where The Dune Grass Ends

I stand now where
the dune grass
ends.

Before me
the beach lies
dappled in
late sun,
a sea itself of
empty footprints.

Beyond,
last waves of
the day
foam and run
up the smooth
wet sand.

An offshore breeze
is gentle
on my back,
the sand cool
to my bare
feet.

Far off
a single sail
recedes
heading for
a horizon
over which
there are,
as yet,
no stars.

I notice that
the pockets of
my jacket are
empty.
I smile,
content
to just stand
there where
the dune grass ends.

Until Then We Wait

The sand is
evening cool
now.

We bury our
bare feet in it
and wait like
the others
looking out

and over
the water to
where the sun
just
went down.

The long shadows
are gone now and
night has invaded
the harbor town
behind us.

The others
rise up to leave
and pass slowly
before us, fading
silhouettes along
the water's edge

We wait.

Soon the water,
holding onto
the warmth of
the day, will be
as still as
this sky.

Then we too
will rise and
go down
to the water's
edge and
further,

for tonight
we will swim
among the stars.

Until then...
we wait.

Of True Depth

Too deep now
to see anything
of bottom,

still we
lean to look
drawn
to probe
dark water,

if for
no other reason
than to
get a sense of
true depth.

To Dark Waters

Just now,
with the last
touch of sun
slipping behind
the dark trees,

a heron,
on wings of
prehistory,
sweeps past and
settles into
its own stillness,

to wait until night
consigns it too
to dark waters.

Coming Back

Coming back, I
search for that
exact spot where
she stood with
eyes closed to
the sea and
the wind.

Coming back, all
I find is sand
smoothed by
the last tide.

Coming back, I
realize that I
can only
approximate,
and that

coming back is
like trying to
build again
yesterday's
sand castle.

This Sea

This sea
does not
beckon
to me now.

Gray as this
sky,

its surface is
impenetrable,
still

I know the
rock strewn
beach that
lies beneath.

Having grown
too tired
to swim and
too heavy
to float
I ask
nothing
of it,
except

to just stand
here at
the water's edge
and watch the
gray waves come
silently in,
bearing nothing.

This New World

It was all
of distance then,

endless and
ever reaching
towards
endlessness,

with
not a footprint
to be seen in
the wet sand.

We knew that
nothing
had ever
come ashore
here.

Mornings
found the world
newborn
and naked then

here at
the edge of
this new world.

Message In A Bottle

This sand,
so white,
becomes in time
so much a
part of
everything
here.

Up beyond
the water's reach
it mixes with
something that
can support
tall grass that
comes up like
dry sabers.

Further on
palms grow
sparsely at first
and then
ever more
densely.

The sea here is
so pure and
so clear that
a long way out
one can still see
the white sand
deep beneath.

During the day
the shadow
of a shark
can be seen
a long way off
and one can swim
without fear.

At night
there is always
the lagoon.

Most days
I walk the shore.
The island is
small enough that
I have come to
know it well.

As I walk
I keep to where
the sea
washes up clean
on the sand,
and I never
come upon
footprints
not even
my own.

Often I just stand
looking out
to where sea
and sky meet,
letting my feet
sink slowly into
the soft sand.

There could be
a wreck out there
somewhere,
but as yet
nothing has
washed ashore.

It's been so long
since I
dismantled and
put to flame
my own
small craft, that
I no longer
remember its
look, color, how
it sailed or
even its name.

It is long since
the breezes
carried its ashes
out to sea.

Its sail
still provides
some degree
of shade
when I sit with
my thoughts
which,
one by one
drift away and
never return.

And then
there is this
one last bottle,
the only thing
left from
somewhere else,
it and
these words.

Forgive me for
not saying more.

Forgive me for
leaving out
longitude and
latitude.

Forgive me but
the sand, you see,
in time
becomes so
much a part
of everything
here.

North Over South

In a car so small
that I can reach
and lock
every door
even as I
drive,

I make my way
each morning
down a highway
that by-passes
the inner city
the lights of which
look so much
at that hour like
somewhere else.

Even after
so many miles
the steering wheel
is still cold
and I can see
my breath.

Over there
to my left
in the east
there is
first light.

It is the first
morning of
November.

At this moment
many latitudes
south, I know
that means
something
very different.

Immersion

Removing
what little
she wore to
the sound of
water
falling into
a small pool,

she made her way
to the outcrop from
which the water
fell, her white feet
gliding softly over
the damp moss.

On hands and feet
she slid along
a slope of rock
and slipped
slowly into the
swirling water,

lowering herself
until her long hair
floated around
her shoulders.

Turning, she
waded towards
the turbulent
water until
its whiteness and
her own were
one.

Reaching ahead
with both hands,
she paused and
then, leaning
forward, she
slipped under
and away,
leaving nothing but
the sound of
water
falling into
a small pool.

Among Old Apples

The tree now
come to this
its own
emptiness,

last apples lie
neglected in
long grass and
long fallen
leaves.

In your hand
you hold
one small and
gnarled and
the color of
something poor,
which
you offer to me.

"Not this time,"
I say with a
stillness that
is now
mine alone.

With a nod
you let
the apple drop
and then sit
beside me on
this low stone wall.

Across the way
the pasture gate
leans ready
to fall.

Beyond it
the hills lose
their evening glory.

It is late.
It is cold.
And the snake has
long moved on leaving
only his slough
among old apples.

Beyond Stained Glass

It is a church
much too large
in its own emptiness
for even one
simple prayer to
fulfill itself.

Statues painted
in primary colors,
with faces more
grim than holy
lurk
in each apse.

The stations
of the cross tell
only the one tale,
one already
too much told.

Alone and kneeling,
I find once again
that the words
of my heart are
somewhere else,

somewhere
out there beyond
the stained glass
where the snow
silently fills
a late afternoon.

Position

It would be
a day back
when the uniforms
were flannel and
the gloves small.

It would be an
afternoon
late and
long given to
gray.

The stands
would by now
be empty
except for you.

That would be
me there
in right field,
the last player left
on the field.

Yes, that
would be me
the player
not listed on
your scorecard,

possibly
the player to
be named later.

Window Shopping

It is all
slush and slick
sidewalk out here.

These shoes are
old and my feet
ache and cramp
with the cold as
I stand out here
looking into this
well lit shop.

You are there on
the other side of
the glass a
table width of
cacti away.

Standing there
I watch as you
consider
each cactus
leaning intently
sometimes
picking one up
to examine it
more closely.

I wait out here
conscious only of
the cold and
the ache and
the cramps
in my feet.

I wait out here
fingering
the change in
my pocket and
calculating
the price of
a cup of coffee
two doors down.

But I still wait.

I wait knowing
how, as always,
you must
take what you
consider to be
ample time
before you choose

the one.

I wait knowing
that you will
finally
decide on one
then reconsider
and then
decide on it
again.

I wait already
knowing what
the final choice
will be, and so
I stand here
waiting
ready to nod
my approval.

Waiting For The Stars

It is a room
large and empty
and right enough for
a ballet troupe.

The windows
are tall
the floorboards
bare and
polished.

Being bare
of furniture
I must sit
cross-legged and
lean forward
to write.

Sitting so low,
all I can make out
through the windows
are the topmost branches
of bare trees
against
a pale sky.

The windows
are closed.

The voices of
children at play
beyond sound
far away.

Opposite the windows
is a bare wall,
long and
tall and painted white.

There is an
immensity to
it's bareness.

They could,
I think,
install
a mirror there,
one the size
of the wall.

Maybe then
dancers would come
and practice hard
and tire.

But then,
knowing nothing
of dance or
dancers or
even how
to dance, I set
the idea free.

Maybe the dancers
would not come.

Maybe
it is better
to just let
a blank wall be.

Maybe
it is better
not to risk
finding myself
alone with
my reflection
in a room
mirrored
to twice
its size.

Maybe
it is best
just to take
what view
a window
affords and
wait
for the stars
to appear.

Something

One solitary
mosquito
could fill a room
as empty
as this,

as could
not much of
a song,

some simple
melody,

or a refrain
repeated
endlessly,

something
drifting through
the open windows,

something that
can caress these
bare walls.

It wouldn't
take much,

a tune at its
most bare, or

one
solitary
mosquito.

Bystanders

Down the street
where the town
ends, a dog,
crazed under a
high noon sun,
dances a
tarantella with
itself in
the dust.

Keeping a
safe distance
we stand unseen
in the shade
ever so careful
not
to wet
our whistles.

Old Photographs

It is nothing more
than a collection of
old photographs taken
over the years,
photographs with
a French
sensibility.

Here, in this one
we have Germans
marching with
their heavy helmets,
their long coats and
and their trombones,

and then, in this one,
they are gone,
leaving nothing
but a void beneath
Le Arc de Triomphe.

And then there is
this last one with
the light of late
afternoon
coming through
the long blinds
to loiter on
the wall above an
unmade bed,

a photograph
that could have been
taken at
any time.

Age

I have seen
the old women
go past in pairs
dressed in their
best black, and

I have noted
how each
holds to
the other.

I have watched
the small matched
steps that
they take to cover
familiar ground.

I have seen
their lips move
as they
confide again
to each other
all that
they have known
for so long.

Seeing them so,
time and
time again,
I have come
to know that
age keeps well
its own counsel.

Friday 12/24 1:00 am

Taking the curve at
18 years of age and
for more arc than
it was worth,

she took down
the young maple
and died,

and mom
in her kerchief
and I
in my cap
could do
nothing at all to
bring her back.

Dorothy

Here
at first light she
stands alone upon
the deck of
a ship that
for her has
come too far.

Through
the long night
she has stood here
turned to
the unseen shore,
her back to
all she will
no longer have.

Here
at first light she
climbs the gunwale
and slips down
into the now
and forever sea.

Comrades

There are others
armed like
myself
making their way
up the long,
steep hill.

Through
the mist
and smoke,
through these
empty trees
I see them and
do my best
to keep pace.

A Darker Soil

The fighting now
having drawn
near enough,
the tank crews
come in each evening
just as
the field hands did
before the war,

and, like them,
they come
all grime and sweat
and drink and
complain about
their day and
their lot in death.

Things are
not that much
different now
except that
during the day
we can hear
the tank crews,
off in the distance,
busy
at their work.

Life During Wartime

Despite the fact
that the fires were
all but spent,
smoke still hung heavy
as if unable, like us,
to escape.

Hidden and waiting
in a street entry
to a basement of
a building
now mostly
gutted, I
count the seconds,

falling back to
one with
each blast, always
hoping to make it
to a thousand,
my arbitrary limit
to danger.

Others, I know,
set other limits
as they hide
beneath tables with
the shades drawn.

Others still, I know
live without
any limits at all
and are now
at this moment
in the square
toppling
mighty statues.

The Slow Ending

It is never just
an external death
alone that is
suffered, but one
where things
long molten within
slowly cool.

It is
the hidden life that
gives way
first.

What comes later
is nothing but
the inevitable, but

it is a death
nevertheless and
it is one that
that reaches
the outermost
orbits with
its touch,

much in the way
a planet will
waste away in
sympathy with
a dying sun.

To Bottom

Falling down
the long stairs,
we pass over
many steps.

Those we hit have
something
of bottom to them.

With each
of those we
learn
a little more,

so that when
the bottom
finally comes
it comes as
no real surprise.

Reaching Back

Ionean or
some sea where
the sand can
still be seen
a pale green
at many fathoms.

Kythira or
some island with
white beaches
hidden in
rocky coves.

Aphrodite or
some other deity
content to
stroll naked in
pure sunlight.

A myth or
some other tale
with which
to amuse myself
in the void.

Acrophobia

Fear does not
follow me up
up this ladder.

Oh no.

Fear is up there
already,
sitting
on the edge with
its feet on
the top-most rung.

It is up there
waiting with
its patient smile.

With each rung
I climb I
hear a little more
clearly
the one word
it has to say in
its wasp-whisper…

"Gravity."

Come With Me

Come with me to
that side of this
great building,
the side that
faces
the wind.

The sun is
that bright enough
today.

Come with me
to the rail and
let us, with our
gloved hands,
hold and
brace ourselves.

The earth spins
fast enough, but
no faster.

Come with me
and listen to
the dark waters
that run against
the large rocks there.

All movement is
both balanced
and equal.

Come with me and
let us measure all
the surfaces where
no foot rests.

Loneliness is
a universal
complaint.

Come with me and
let us share
those songs that
we have learned
elsewhere from
others.

Everyone
that you know
knows
someone else.

Come with me and
breathe air brave
enough to make
seagulls soar.

This moment is
the smallest portion
of enternity.

Come with me, just
come with me and
let us go.

*For every need
there is a
perceived
satisfaction.*

Born Too Late

The City of New York has printed tourist guides for its newest attraction: Staten Island's Fresh Kills Landfill. Sanitation workers turned tour guides will follow a 30 page script to point out the various sights such as the cranes which unload barges full of trash 24 hours a day. " There seems to be an increasing demand for tours," insists deputy landfill director William Cloke (AP).

As a young lad
I often road past the site
with my family
on our weekly,
Sunday trips
to visit grandparents.

Even back then
there were mighty cranes
loading, literally,
mountains of
city garbage
on to barges
as big as islands.

At one time it was
the last resting place
of old ships,
tugs and barges
(some circa WWI)
beached and
rotting away.

As a young lad
my father used to
play and swim
among them,
back in what
we always called
the good old days.

On Safari

Try as I might
I have yet to sight
the lion among
the water lilies.

In the still water
I see the clouds
that pass overhead
and the pale blue
between them.

Deeper still
I can make out
the small stones
and sand that
make up the bottom.

But...
try as I might...
no lion.

Still I sit
ready to sight
the lion among
the water lilies,
a king to me
as real as
any thought given
life through words.

Here

Here
the land is one of
fine, fine sand.
Everything slips
easily through
one's fingers.

Here
the low dunes
slope gently.
One step
is little higher
than any other.

Here
the breeze whispers
softly.
One must listen
with intent.

Here
The melody is
aeolian.
An anthem that
has no words.

Here
the tide
never varies.
Time
stands
still.

Here
the horizon
is the limit
no matter where
one stands.
Nothing
can approach
unseen.

Here
it is a paradise,
an Eden
at it's most
austere.

It Ends

It was
a turning rain
that came
in the night
and lasted until
first light.

It came
with a wind that
filled the trees,
stripping them of
what it could and
leaving only the litter
of blow-down and
a sense of loss,
of what cannot
be retrieved.

Nothing
is left now
that speaks of
the season past.

Nothing
is left now
save reminders
rendered past
and imperfect by
a turning rain.

No Remainder

Little gets
tossed
anymore.

Coffee grounds.
The core and seeds
of the pepper.
The skin of the garlic.
The butt
of the carrot.

So little
in fact that
come Wednesday
the trash bag
is no longer
quite full.

So it tends
to be when
the equation becomes
only divisible
by one.

Indulgence

Each morning, after
a pre-dawn run
a shower
a glass of milk and
one package of
Pop-Tarts…

Each morning, after
all of that and
before everything
and everyone else…

he allows himself
the luxury of
those few minutes
necessary for
a game of
solitaire,

taking the result as
neither prophecy for
nor precursor of
what may transpire
that day,

but rather one of
acquiescence to
and a reminder that
the shuffle is always
the determinant,
both unknown and
unknowable,

and that when
the dealer
is no one
but oneself,
cheating is
futile,

and that
win or lose
means less than
just facing
each card as
it is turned.

THE
SONNETS

Musing

She sits upon this bank of moss, alone,
here now to gaze into this sylvan pool,
and gain a sense of distance arboreal
through which these dark waters have run.

With legs drawn up and wrapped within her arms,
she feels beyond the passing time, and smiles.
Content with thoughts her own, their lack of guile,
she slips deeply into the moment's charms.

And unaware of someone drawing near
one following the stream intent upon
the flow, the way the water wanders on,
who stops when he espies her sitting there.

And, turning, draws away with a quickness
so as not to play Pan to her Pitys.

(from a sculpture by Christopher Gowell)

Saint Sebastian

They say the men at arms made much of you
and loosed their arrows without restraint
until you fell into a deathly faint.
Their arrows spent, task done, they withdrew.

Another archer, Eros (maybe) by
name, beheld the widow of Castulus,
Irene, and sent a single shaft that thrust
Into her heart. She fell, but not to die,

only to live and love again. It was she
who plucked you dead and nursed you back to
life, only to have you martyred anew,
clubbed to death, once and for all. So you see

you may be born again without complaint
but you must die again to be a saint.

(from a sculpture by Christopher Gowell)

Summer Wind

It was on turning once again towards shore
to where the only world she ever knew
remained, she felt the summer wind anew
and paused to glance back and to wait before

proceeding on. It was as if she heard
a gentle summons from somewhere beyond
or whisper of what was but now was gone
or a silent prayer without a single word.

It was as if with copper and with tin
wrest from some hidden mine in the Levant
or Persian plateau equally distant
she knew herself cast over once again.

And so the summer wind was not at fault
nor was Lot's wife when she had turned to salt.

(from a sculpture by Steven Carpenter)

HAIKU

across the bay
distant lights soft in
tonight's mist

                    the tea water murmurs
                    the tea pot whistles
                    the tea

driving in night rain
a toad turns out
to be a leaf

on the wet road
beneath an empty tree
bright leaves

beneath the streetlamp
a picket fence
its peeling paint

under the top sheet
watching the ceiling fan
together

frozen grapes
rubies
for dessert

THE VINEYARD

beneath a red sun
a horse feeds
on wet grass

                  between twin suns
                  the light mist
                  on Seth's Pond

from Makonikey shade
the Elizabeth Islands
bright with first light

beyond the scrub oak
the rolling surf
the rounding stones

while seagulls hover
cloud shadows race
down the beach

above the bent
beach umbrellas
a plane comes in low

two women in
black, one piece suits
go only knee deep

here she comes again
the Amazon
in the orange two piece

on a small ankle
lotion, sand and
rainbow thread

past lunch
a seagull stalking among
the sleeping bathers

at low tide
walking far enough
to make first footprints

a gutted dog fish
around the eyes
flies gather

by the honeysuckle
a rainbow of
Adirondack chairs

Taylor's porch
beach towels and
bathing suits

FLORIDA

wading, buoyed by
Gulf waters and
a waning moon

condo pool
raindrops and
raisin fingers

tropical gale
deck chairs
in the pool

after the storm
a young boy
and his puddle

perched on the top
of the tallest tree
an ibis

shell hash
the crunch beneath
my sandals

aeolian transport
a ghost crab
stands his ground

white caps
the luff in
my beach shirt

beneath palm sway
lizards as still
as forgotten toys

winter tides
the sands
reconfigure

                    that first sip
                    iced coffee
                    over salty lips

out there on the Gulf
it is still a night
with heat lightning

a piling gone to rot
still perch enough
for a pelican

surfacing,
time, she says,
for a water hug

condo pool
churning laps before
the heat sets in

ghost crab
presence
then absence

                              cloud morphs
                              see that dog there
                              it's Snoopy

polarized clouds
looking like
album cover art

wading to shore
the taste of salt
on my moustache

storm wrack
as dry as
an old memory

yards from shore
as if floating
two large, ladies hats

a rainbow umbrella
cartwheels
down the beach

lanai railing
beach towels
and bathing suits

Anna Maria Island where
a ghost crab's home
is his sand castle

across these
Gulf waters
a fading Buck Moon

            back from the beach
            the taste of salt
            on her cool skin

from far off
a train whistle
The Tropicana Express

behind the angler
a blue heron
bides its time

                              walking the scarp line
                              setting off
                              small avalanches

up by the dunes
fresh wrack, thoughts
of last night's storm

the pull of
celestial gravity
on my inner sea

late morning
a blossoming of
beach umbrellas

beyond the buoys
a cavorting
of dolphins

a new beach beauty
dark shades
and diaper

skimmers
strafing the surface
keep your head down

Florida roads
beware
of Buicks

the Gulf all breakers
her words drowned
in the roar

on the sandbar
a United Nations
of the avian world

the roar of the waves
the ballet of
the sea oats

studying sea hash
a mosaic
from a mermaid

a bait boat hugs
the morning shore
its crew of egrets

out by the buoys
we swim with
the dolphins

these old oaks
their beards of
Spanish Moss

                              after Hermine
                              coconuts
                              among the wrack

salad for dinner
for dessert
a thunderstorm

on wet sand
a horse-shoe crab
thoughts of Jersey

        in the runnel
        a white heron and
        a white heron reflected

low full moon
the beach about as wide
as it can be

the northern end of
Anna Maria Island, between
sunrise and moon set

beyond Egmont Key
one ship arrives as
another departs

a black moon night
the beach littered
with dead fish

at the masque
of the red tide
the ghost crabs feast

a sky of stars
above this redolence
of red tide

a hunting party
a tern shadowed
by a crow

cloud shadows race
down the beach
as mine stands watching

           onshore wind
           piling waves
           tumbleweeds of froth

red tide
at the high water mark
turkey vultures stalk

winter white
a pelican flies by
my hood is up

among the shell hash
fragments of sand dollars
Old Neptune's spare change

morning, fog bound,
waves rolling in
from nowhere

walking the beach
in dense morning fog
phantoms approach

pictures drawn
in this wet sand
this etch-a-sketch

in wet sand
hearts, arrows, initials
Valentine's Day

Easter morning
from the deep
a dolphin rises

sea froth, blown ashore,
trimmings from
Neptune's beard

on the bedroom blind
the climbing silhouette
of a wasp

summer rain
the wipers on
intermittent

Sunday, stopping
to read a prayer
written in wet sand

early morning walk
a sand castle haunted
by a ghost crab

walking slowly along
the boy plays catch
with himself

high humidity
this horde of clouds
advances

almost Christmas
the fragrance of
burning orange peels

BASEBALL

Vintage Baseball
thinking of
my father's smile

                                  once again
                                  unpacking my glove
                                  its leather stiff

Old Timer's Day
Joe D, swinging
for the fences

broken bat single
so much for
my lucky bat

crowding
under the umbrella
rain delay

top of the fifth
thunder
closing in

safe at first
bat sting
in his hands

LONESOME LAKE

on this fine autumn day
Lonesome Lake Trail
isn't

                              hands-a-pockets
                              just letting my feet
                              find their way

between the rocks
the yellow leaves
the dark earth

up high now
walking along
the treetops

stopping to wait
for my daughter's voice
to catch up

back down
at trail's end
red leaf litter

behind me
fallen leaves
forgotten haiku